Changing the Energy

Cate Pickup

BookLeaf Publishing

Presentation by *BookLeaf Publishing*

Web: www.bookleafpub.com

E-mail: info@bookleafpub.com

ISBN: 9789358310085

First edition 2023

DEDICATION

To my boys, Jonathan and Adam. Thank you for inspiring me to never give up.

ACKNOWLEDGEMENT

There are so many people I would like to recognize at this time. Without the support of my family, I would never have had the courage to write this book;

Jym—the ultimate dream chaser. Thank you for watching over me as the words flowed from pen to paper.

Sue—thank you for being my friend—and Barb—for never knowing what to say.

AJ - for always bringing your energy.

My boys, for always teaching me something new about myself.

And most importantly my husband, Jason. Without you this book would not have happened.

PREFACE

As I began to write this particular collection of poetry, I sat down to think about what and who had influenced and inspired me throughout the past few years. My writings are my interpretation of emotions felt in a specific time and place. These experiences have incorporated their energies into my life in some way. Writing this collection has been a journey of my soul. I hope they provide some insight into my experiences, both challenging and rewarding, and you are able to draw your own positive energy from it.

The Pyramid

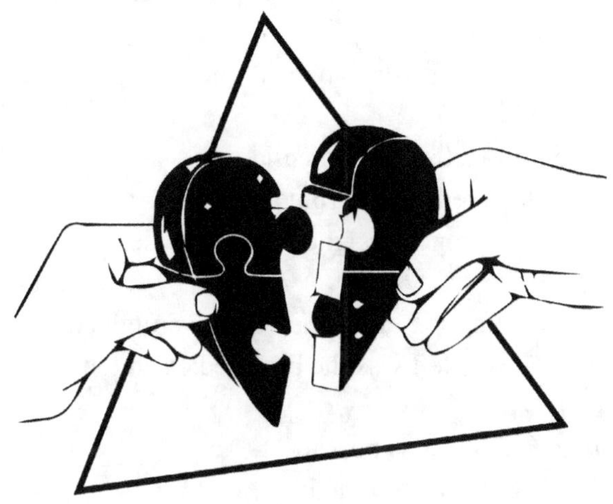

Long ago the pyramid was built
A pyramid of virtue to the gods
Created from carefully placed stones
Each stone telling a story of the future
And each had its own hidden past

The stones contained stories of the gods and
their offspring
One stone tells of a son exiled for lack of
sacrifice to the gods
One stone tells of a son considered the village
idiot

One stone tells of a daughter possessed by
demons
One stone tells of a son who walked among the
gods
One stone tells of a daughter who lived in fear of
the gods
One stone tells of a lost child
One stone tells of a forbidden love
All of the stones designed to fit together

As the offspring grew, their stones crumbled
All that was left was the base dedicated to the
gods
Judgement Day is nearing
The base began to crumble
The gods will also be judged

Found Faith

It was in the air
It descended from heaven on the wings of angels
It was a spirit of life
It was new to her
Her soul rose up to meet it

Together, spirit and soul transcended the body
The tension was gone
The heart was no longer weighed down
It was light and free
This spirit filled the body
A smile replaced the once constant frown
A sparkle shone through her eyes
It transformed her
She walked on air
Her worries left her
An inner strength started to emerge
Her faith had been restored.

The Invisible Connection

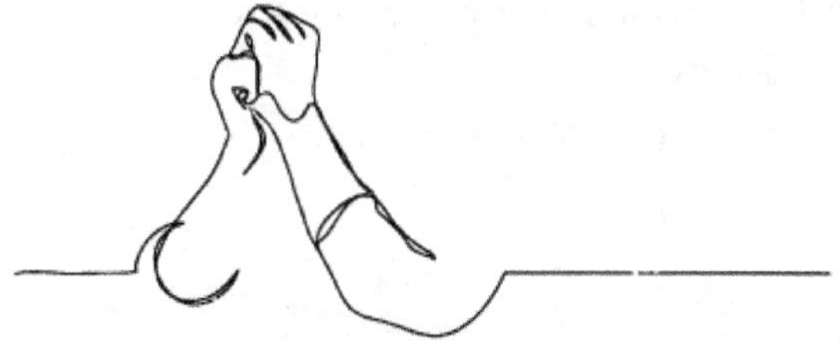

It's eerie how similar they are
Yet there are a world of differences
Born years and miles apart
Somehow it was like they were separated at
birth
Same personalities, one quiet and reserved, the
other outgoing and affectionate
They closely resemble each other
Yet no lineage to connect them
How is that possible?
It is as if the unlinked ancestors were reborn

Sent to this place to provide comfort to the next
in line
Brought together by a chance conversation
Connected by a complete stranger
It is far from a coincidence
There is only one possibility, and one subtle
answer
A heavenly angel directed their path
Guided by her hand
To be received by the lonely one

Conversations with Flowers

Good morning, Gorgeous
Look at you
So bright and vibrant
Keep it up; you are beautiful

Hello Beautiful
You seem to be having a down day
Let's get rid of that dead weight holding you
back
You've got this all day!

Hey Gorgeous
Let's get you some water
It's important to stay hydrated
It will keep you feeling refreshed inside and out

Good evening, Beautiful
You've had a full day soaking in the sun
It's time to rest for the evening
You need to remember to take care of yourself.

Change

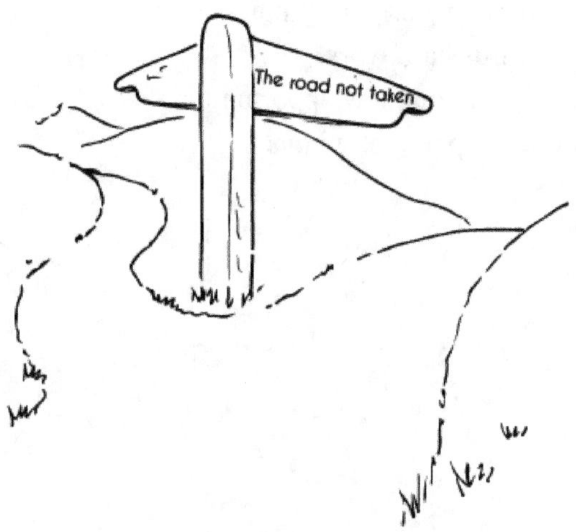

Change
It takes effort
It requires a desire for a different outcome
It demands for an uncomfortableness to be
welcomed
It insists on calling into questions all norms

Change
It breaks you down
It cracks foundations that have been solid for
generations

It keeps coming relentlessly
It slows down for no one and nothing

Change
It promises a brighter future
It rewards hard work
It brings about new opportunities
It opens up a light within.

Pandora's Box

An unmarked box
There it sat next to the recliner
Unassuming
What was inside
A lifetime of love
An eternity of pain
Memories of days gone by
Love letters saved from anniversaries past
Dreams and promises of a brighter tomorrow
Favorite sweatshirts and treasured trinkets
Memories of holidays and cherished moments

Sorrows of a life now breathless
Grief for the one dearly missed
All gently placed with love and purpose
To keep company next to the recliner
An unmarked box.

For My Mom

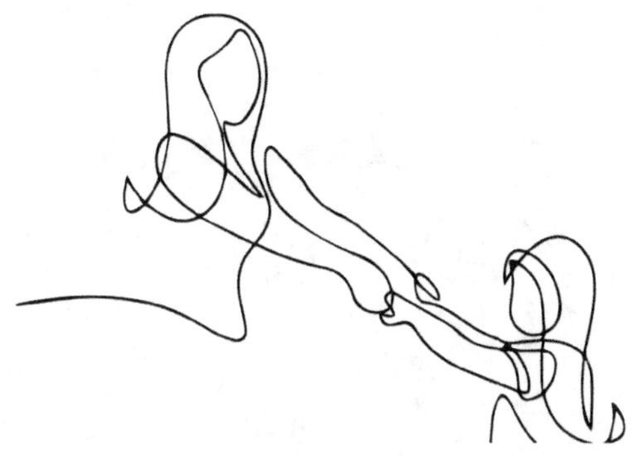

She is the song of the birds singing outside the
window
She is the fragrance of the flowers hanging in
the sunlight
She is the melody of the of the wind chimes that
dangle in the breeze
She is the peacefulness of the frogs chirping in
the dusk
She is the song on the radio that evokes a
memory down the cheek
She is the warmth in the blanket gifted long ago
She is the smell of freshly baked cookies hot
from the oven
She is the sparkle in the lake glistening from the
sun
She is the star shining bright in the evening sky
She is my mom, and I miss her.

My Everything

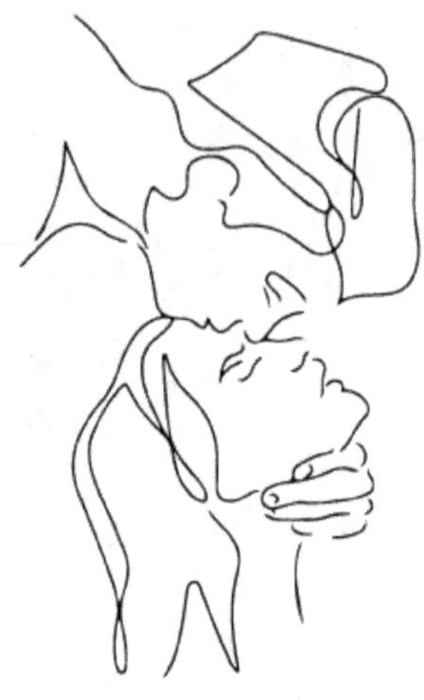

Forehead kisses
Hugs from behind
Unexpected flowers
Slow dances in the grocery store
Last minute adventures
Questions of "Why are you so tiny?"
Somewhere between 16 to 18
Twist my arm he says
Eyes you get lost in
A soul sensitive to touch
Peacefulness in his arms
Easy much like a Sunday morning
Listening may not be his strongest suit
But he loves the hell outta me,

The Most Natural High

The music starts to play
It hits every soul in earshot
Air drums begin deafening the room
Anticipation fills the atmosphere

As the seconds pass by, the energy level rises
The king is nearing his arrival
The crowd calls to him feverishly
MDK MDK MDK

At last the time has come

The curtain throws open, the god is here!
All at once the mass of the many become one
Surrounding the king, the one from Eastern
Block

No one is immune to the excitement that
blankets the room
Moshing with the god
Firing him up as he ascends to his throne
It is MDK all freakin day.

The Ballad of the Bulldozer

Art imitating life's emotions
Shattered glass, a shattered heart
Shards lie everywhere in a million pieces
Impossible to be made whole again
The only way to get through the pain is to feel
more pain
Begging for more, knowing that more agony is
to coming
Because nothing else exists
The world is void of all other feelings
Everything else ceased when the light went out
It sucked the last breath of air out of itself

To survey the darkness is to embrace the
violence
There was no light waiting on the other side, just
a new existence
The brutality slowly escalated, covering him like
a cocoon
No butterfly will emerge from the shell
Only a being reborn in the void of life.

The Dream Chaser

Once there was a guy whose name was Jym
Jym was a friendly fellow,always had a smile for
everyone
To know Jym was to love him
You couldn't help it, even when he made
mistakes

Jym had a puppy personality, soft and loving
Someone you enjoyed being around
Always helped the ones he loved, but good at
letting them down

And even then, you still loved him

Jym lived for himself, chasing his dreams no
matter the cost
There was no convincing him otherwise
He lived with the price tag carrying it with him
inside

Jym is no longer with us, it hurts everyday
A best friend to all, a brother to those special
few
The day we lost him the world went dark
We learn to live without his laugh, his hugs

Jym, we know you watch over us all to this day
in angel form you show us in your own way
Your life had meaning, a purpose
For you showed others ow to love and be loved
Rest easy, until we meet again.

Heart Break

It was an unexpected journey for him
Caught him off guard with little time to process
You are so young, they would say to him
Good that we caught it now

Go to the doctor, she said. it will be good, she
said
Half joking, half serious he mocked his wife
Never letting his emotions show as he jumped
Hoop after hoop, needles and tests and more
needles

The big day was finally here

He walked into the building, seemingly matter
of fact
He checked in, and she waited anxiously
The time came to part ways

She watched him walk down the hall alone
She thought about how brave he was, facing this
on his own
She felt helpless, wanting to be with him
On the bench outside, she cried, scared of losing
her world

The hours, the minutes, they passed so slow
Praying and hoping to get word soon
At last the phone rang
Her prayers were answered, he made it through.

Unprepared

I thought I was ready for it
I joked that I had trained for it
Growing up alone, isolated in a remote area
Not seeing anyone for days on end? Been there,
done that
Few options at the grocery store? No sweat
Limit your time near others? story of my life
What I didn't expect - the mental toll
Not of the pandemic, but the rush of feelings of
days past
I didn't realize until I was already consumed

The lack of confidence, the constant questioning
The uncertainty of everything, it flooded my
soul
As life slowly returned to normal, I was stuck
Stuck in a place that held on like thick mud
The past had caught up with me
The overthinking went into overdrive
I thought I was ready for it
No one can or should train for that experience

Serenity

She sat high on the hill
Overlooking the glistening lake
The warm breeze gently blowing
The sun shining down on her
Mountains in every direction as far as you could
see

It was the most peaceful place she could find
She would get lost in the sparkling waves
No one else around but the ancestors of the land
Daydreaming of a better life

It was her escape from the anxious chaos
That suffocated her every breath
For a while nothing could touch her
She was in her own world

She found her sanctuary here
The feeling of serenity would embed itself into
her soul
Years later she would call upon it
Remembering her time high on the hill

Grief Comes

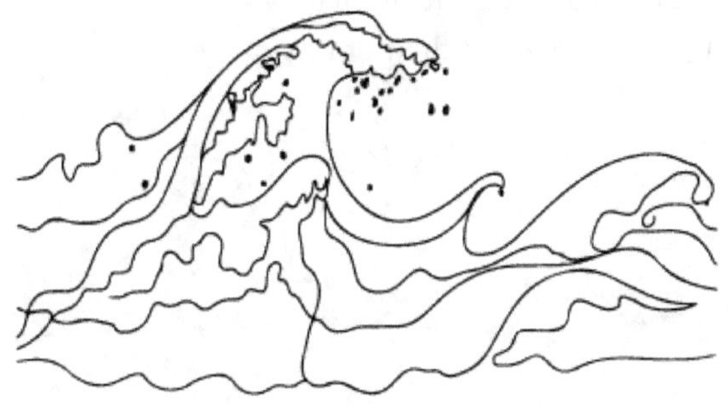

In the car thinking about past family holidays
Looking through old photographs
Watching a tv show they used to watch together
The smell of a candle wafting through the air
When one of their favorite songs comes on the
radio
When you see them in your kids as they get
older
When you are having a tough day and need a
hug
Making an old family favorite recipe

In the middle of the night when memories keep
you from sleeping
As you plant flowers in the springtime
The one movie that always made them laugh
When you are cleaning
On the way to work
In challenges left incomplete
When you stare at their empty chair

Energy

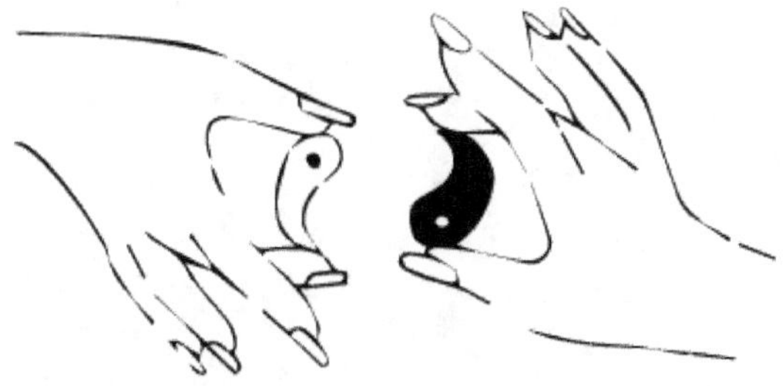

Energy is all around us
It is unavoidable
In the laughter of children playing
In the melody of a sad song
In the purr of a sleepy kitten
In the bark of an excited pup
Filling a room with folks celebrating
Surrounding those in despair and grieving
Our souls feed off of it
Absorbing the energy it encounters
It's in the flowers reaching for the sun

In the ducks swimming peacefully in the pond
It's in the mountains, protecting the valley
Energy - it's all around us.

Attack of Anxiety

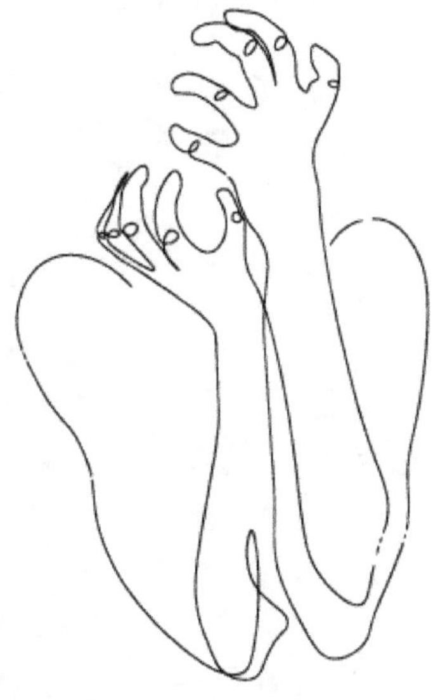

It creeps up on you
Like a shadow in the sunlight
Integrating into every fiber of the being
Slowly taking over
Holding on with a cramped grip
Chest tightening, panicked and overwhelmed
Unable to think straight
Overcoming all of the senses
The only sound is the unspoken voice
Pulse racing yet incapable of moving
Like an engine stuck in neutral

Revving up but going nowhere
Trapped in a house of mirrors that has no way
out
Drowning in a sea of self doubt

Moving Forward

One day, one moment at a time
Sitting back and surveying the landscape
What does it look like
What can it look like
How to get it to that future state

So much to consider, to contemplate
Easier said than done
Moving forward comes with change
Status quo is no longer
But isn't that the objective?

With change comes growth
Growth doesn't happen overnight
It takes dedication, determination
Believing in the ultimate outcome
Even when it seems impossible

She

She fights like a fierce warrior in the darkest of
battles
She plays like a young child in a simpler time
She lends help to others in times of need
She does not know the meaning of surrender
While her mind plays tricks, trying to deceive
her
She focuses on listening only to her positive
alter
She whispers to animals befriending all she can
She talks to flowers, bringing them to life

She fights her inner demons determined to win
She feels the angels who fly near
She loves deeply and soulfully
She seeks knowledge and understanding
She is worthy and enough
One day soon, she will believe this.

The End

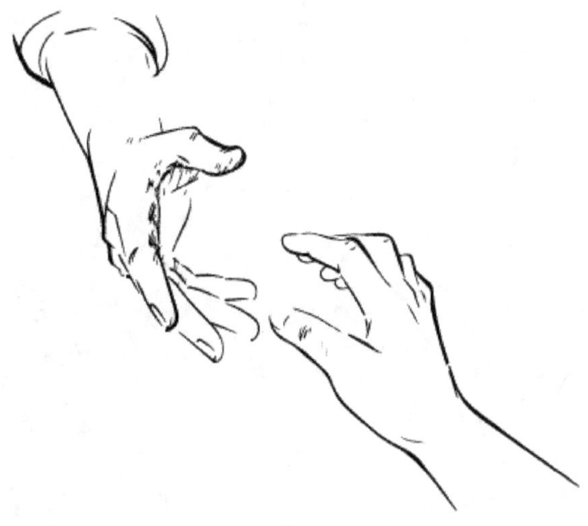

Time is lost, unable to retrieve
And now he is gone
Words left unspoken, unheard
Where to go from here

Complicated feelings, leave the soul numb
Tears fall with unclear meaning
Trying to process seems unattainable
If only this was not how it ended

Unsure of what to hold onto
Too many questions left unanswered
The ending cannot be rewritten
The curtain has closed on the finale.

Love Story

Better together
Through space and time
Have I told you lately
That I love you
You can tell me again
I freaking love you
Stronger on the other side
To the moon for the third time
Forever connected, no matter the distance
Believing in each other
Being honest with each other

Building together, growing together
The realest of love stories.

40

www.ingramcontent.com/pod-product-compliance
Lightning Source LLC
LaVergne TN
LVHW050947200726

843508LV00011B/2463